Understanding Tea

The Essential Guide Series

by Steve Myers

ISBN: 978-0-9934169-2-7

5th Edition 2014
Published by Team Focus Limited, 13 Bridge Street, Maidenhead, Berkshire, SL6 8LR, England
www.teamfocus.co.uk
Tel: +44 (0)1628 637338.

Contents

Overview of Type Mapping

Type Mapping charts the terrain that increases motivation and transforms performance. It is an integrated system based on one powerful model that shines a light on areas often left unmapped. This involves individuals (their preferences, identity and aspirations), situations (the context, demands and challenges) and a focus on the space in-between (interaction, behaviour and relationships). The methods involve 5 lenses which allow for enormous flexibility in terms of intervention and development.

The powerful model underpinning Type Mapping is C.G. Jung's theory of Psychological Types. This theory now provides the mechanism for hundreds of applications that go beyond existing psychometric approaches in two ways.

Firstly, it captures the spirit of Jung's theory by focusing on how a person continues to grow and develop over their life span (i.e. recognising that one's Type can change):

> "Even though assignment to a particular type may in certain cases have lifelong validity, in other very frequent cases it is so dependent on so many external and internal factors that the diagnosis is valid only for certain periods of time" Jung, 1957, p. 347

Secondly it acknowledges that people express themselves in a variety of ways which are dependent on both short-term and long-term environmental experiences.

The Type Mapping wheel provides a simple way to map the territory. To begin the journey there are five different questionnaires as follows:

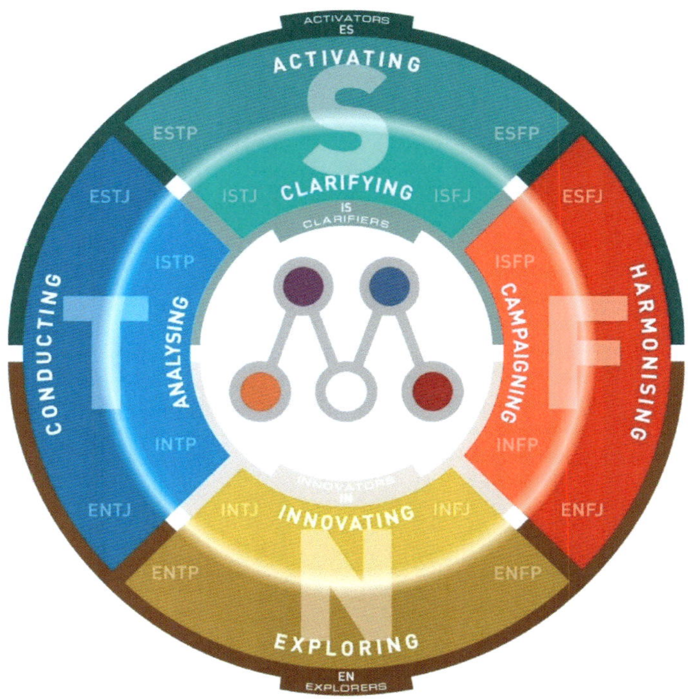

Learning style (LSI™ – the Learning Styles Indicator™)

- **Identity** (TDI® – the Type Dynamics Indicator® – IS version)
- **Aspirations** (TDI-WANT™, the Type Dynamics Indicator® – WANT version)
- **Roles/behaviours** (MTR-i™ – the Managing Team Roles-indicator™)

- **Contextual demand** (ITPQ™ – the Ideal Task Profile Questionnaire™)

In summary, each of these questionnaires explores different space – the inside with the complexities of identity and aspiration which can make the identification of preference difficult; the outside and the situational demands and pressures that require attention; the in-between, which is how we adapt to the differing demands of circumstances and our sense of self.

The roles are described using verbs (gerunds) and the preferences use the 4-letter typology so that there is less confusion between "doing and being". Psychological Type Theory links these elements through the concept of dominant and auxiliary functions (see Briggs Myers 1980).

Each questionnaire can be used on its own for a range of applications. For example, the Type Mapping learning styles (LSI) bear a strong resemblance to Kolb's learning styles (suggesting, in turn, that what Kolb tapped into was psychologically deep and enduring). There are many applications of learning styles, from building self-awareness to developing training programmes, and it can even be used as a way to identify how best to introduce an individual or a group to a Type programme.

Another example is using the MTR-i which can be used to identify multiple roles – an acknowledgement that we all need to and are able to stretch outside our type. Since this can be both exhilarating and stressful, identifying the roles we play enables us to explore our ability to adapt far more easily – adaptation was one of Jung's key concerns.

A further example is using the ITPQ which can be used to identify and understand the organisational culture, or the differing or competing demands and expectations being placed on a team or individual. All of us need to respond to circumstances such as customers, senior management, budgetary restraint and other people but we do not always see clearly what those demands really are.

The real power of the Type Mapping system emerges when these instruments and concepts are used as entry points into a programme that relates two or more of the concepts together. For example, the relationship between preference (TDI-Is) and role (MTR-i) can highlight the 'stretch' that one is currently experiencing in a particular role. Using the TDI-Want can help identify whether such stretch is likely to be stressful or exhilarating. Adding in the ITPQ examines the fit between oneself and the demands on one's role.

The Type Mapping System recognises the complexity and richness of psychological type theory and provides an orientation framework to begin to understand the inner and outer landscapes. It provides a 'matrix' out of which each individual, group or organisation can begin to build their own unique and complex story, and thereby begin to understand some of the many internal and external factors with which they have to grapple.

Introduction to the Team Role Model

People perform a range of roles in their work and in their life. Some of these roles are natural and easy, others can be more unnatural and even difficult. The Team Role descriptions presented in this booklet are a way of capturing the diverse roles, behaviours and contributions in the form of a simple but comprehensive model. This model has been derived from Jung's theory of Psychological Type. This theory suggests some basic psychological functions – or mental muscles – that lead to characteristic styles of behaviour. Whilst everyone can choose to perform/exhibit a wide range of such behaviours, it is unlikely that they will be equally proficient (or practiced) in all of them.

"People clearly have different preferences but, with sufficient motivation, they can stretch to perform any role – and this stretch can be stimulating but can sometimes be stressful"

Team Role theory proposes that the role that people take in any particular context is dependent on both their natural preferences and capabilities influenced by situational demands. Thus people may take one role in one team and a different role in another. In other words people can be flexible about the roles they play. However, they are not always as flexible as they could or should be and they are not always aware of their patterns of behaviour – and how appropriate they are for the context. For this reason, the MTR-i (Managing Team Roles Indicator) helps people recognise what they do/contribute in a specific context. Using Jung's theory of Psychological Type, the interaction between context, behaviour and personality can be identified, analysed, explored and developed to make contributions more flexible and appropriate.

To appreciate the model further it is important to recognise the difference between preference and usage. This can be illustrated by writing your name with your preferred hand, and then writing it again with your other hand. Although this exercise is often used by trainers to illustrate that you have a clear preference for one hand, it also illustrates that you can – and do – use both hands. In fact, for many everyday tasks - such as eating a meal, driving a car, or playing golf - you have to use both hands at the same time and coordinate their use. Also, the hands you use are sometimes different to your preferences, for example the hand you use to change gear whilst driving depends solely on the design of the car and not your preference.

In a similar way, although you probably have a preference for certain mental muscles, as indicated by the TDI Is questionnaire, you use all of those mental muscles. The MTR-i questionnaire helps you identify which mental muscles you are currently using in a particular context, and the type of contribution you are making to your work team. The mental muscles are:

Sensing, which shapes things or information to reflect known experience: taking action to produce tangible outcomes, or clarifying information so that it can be more clearly understood.

Intuition, which sees new patterns and potential in things, people or ideas: changing the way things are done to see if something new & better can be found, or dreaming up new, innovative ideas.

Thinking, which introduces a logical structure into the team's work or analysis: systematising the way things are done, or producing mental models that explain how the world works.

Feeling, which assigns value to people, things, ideas or information: building harmony and team spirit, or stressing the importance of certain ideas or beliefs.

Each of these mental muscles can be used in one of two ways. Both ways involve creating, changing or achieving things, but that change or achievement takes place in one of two worlds:

- the **outer** world of people and things, or
- the **inner** world of ideas and information

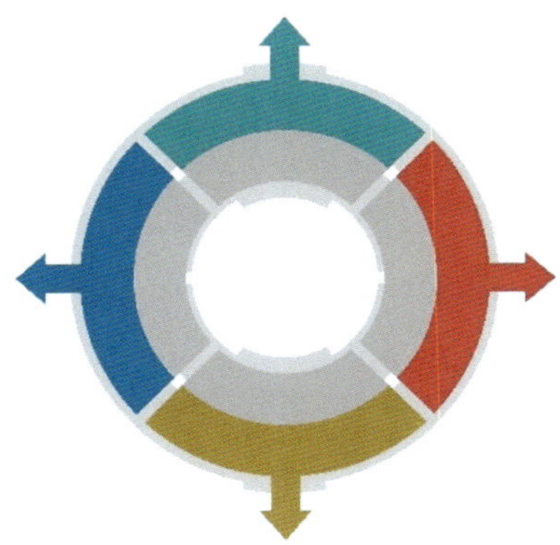

Extraverted Team Roles

When a mental muscle is used in order to change some aspect of the outer world then the mental muscle is "extraverted". Extraverted team roles appear on the outside of the MTR-i team wheel.

Such outer-world roles often involve taking action, discussing things with people, or interacting with machinery. For example, the purpose of a sales discussion is to 'make the sale', to make the customer do something, say 'yes' and sign the order form. Another example might be answering the telephone on a customer care help-line: the aim is to solve the customer's problem, resolve the complaint, and leave the customer feeling satisfied with the service they have received. These are examples of changes being made in the 'outer world'. Other examples include running a training course, chairing a meeting or nursing someone in poor health.

Introverted Team Roles

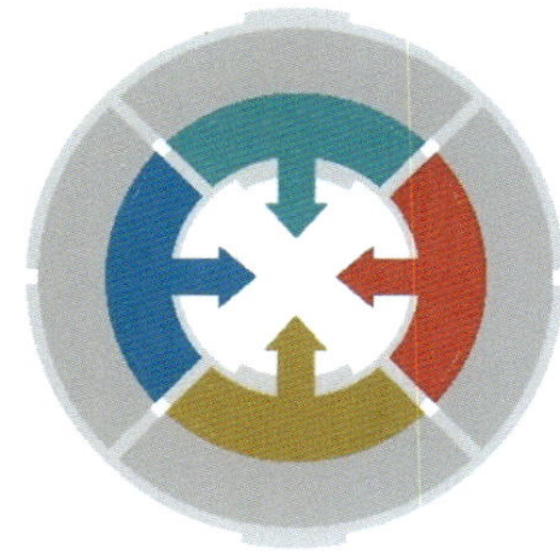

When a mental muscle is used in order to change some aspect of the inner world of ideas or information, then the mental muscle is “introverted”. The team roles on the inside of the team wheel are introverted. Such roles involve making changes to one's own thoughts or understanding, the product of which is information, or ideas.

For example, the purpose of analysing sales statistics may be to identify the most profitable markets or products. This leads to clearer knowledge, or a better understanding, which is an ‘inner world’ product. Other examples of introverted products include: clarifying a customer’s requirements, anticipating future needs, working out how a computer program works, or focusing on the most important thing in a list of tasks.

There is one potential drawback of inner world products: they are not immediately apparent to others, because we have no way of reading each other’s minds. In order for the team to gain the benefit from introverted team roles the ideas, information or understanding that has been generated has to be articulated. This is often done either by discussion during team meetings, or the creation of some written record, such as a report or email.

Overview

When the four mental muscles (Sensing, Intuition, Thinking and Feeling) are combined with the two orientations (extraversion and introversion), the result is eight team roles.

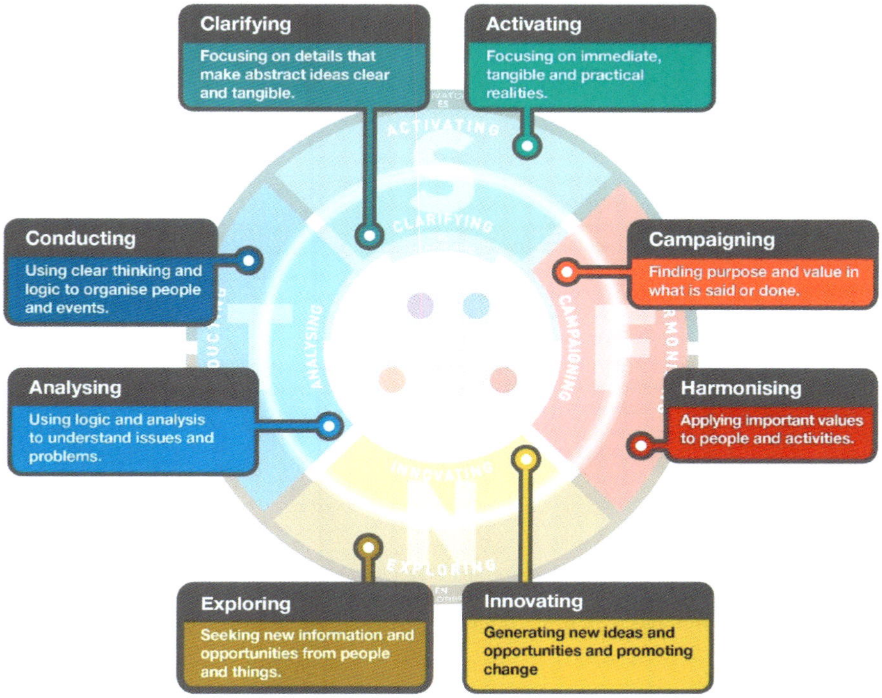

CLARIFYING (Sensing directed to the inner world)

When someone is Clarifying, they are bringing clarity to the inner world of information, ideas and understanding. Clarifying involves listening, asking questions and absorbing information, to achieve as clear a picture or understanding as is possible. Clarifying involves expanding knowledge, collecting experiences, and looking to the foreseeable future by envisaging clear goals and clear pathways to achievement of those goals. The focus on clarity also brings greater attention to detail.

ANALYSING (Thinking directed to the inner world)

When someone is Analysing, they produce explanations of how and why things happen. Analysing brings structure and organisation into the inner world of ideas and understanding. It involves formulating hypotheses and explanations of how things function, and gathering evidence to assess how true those explanations are. Analysing also produces mental models that replicate how particular aspects of the world work, and tries to understand the full complexity of any situation.

INNOVATING (Intuition directed to the inner world)

When someone is Innovating they use their imagination to create radically new and different ideas or perspectives. Innovating delves into the vast pool of ever-changing ideas and images that exist within the unconscious mind, producing radical solutions to problems, a long-term vision and an apparent understanding of the unknown. Innovating also involves observing the world, but using the imagination to consider what is observed from a number of alternative perspectives.

CAMPAIGNING (Feeling directed to the inner world)

When someone is Campaigning, they give importance to particular thoughts, ideas, or beliefs. The mental process of campaigning is value driven, and in a team discussion Campaigning often brings a sense of priority that is derived from strong convictions. Campaigning seizes upon and emphasises ideas or thoughts that have the greatest import, bringing them to the fore and stressing their significance. Campaigning evaluates the inherent value or importance of new ideas, focusing on those that stimulate the strongest feelings.

HARMONISING (Feeling directed to the outer world)

When someone is Harmonising, they try to create harmony in the world around them, by building rapport with people, creating a positive team atmosphere, looking after people's welfare, motivating people and/or providing a service to the satisfaction of others. Harmonising values people's contributions, seeks to develop the role that others play, and invests a lot of effort in building positive relationships. Harmonising tries to overcome differences of opinion and find ways in which the team can agree.

EXPLORING (Intuition directed to the outer world)

When someone is Exploring, they try out new and better ways of doing things, to uncover hidden potential in people, things or situations. They break new ground, and are often looking one step beyond the current situation to pursue unexplored avenues, until all the possibilities have been exhausted. Exploring often challenges the status quo whilst experimenting with the introduction of change, to see if the situation can be improved or new potential uncovered.

CONDUCTING (Thinking directed to the outer world)

When someone is Conducting, they introduce organisation and a logical structure into the way things are done. Conducting involves organising and systematising the world, establishing appropriate plans, identifying and implementing the correct procedures, and then endeavouring to make sure they are followed. Conducting tries to ensure that roles and responsibilities are properly defined and that appropriate resources or skills are available to undertake the work assigned.

ACTIVATING (Sensing directed to the outer world)

When someone is Activating they are bringing things to fruition by getting things done, and getting them done now! Activating is very action-oriented, dealing with whatever tasks the current situation presents, and spurring others into action as well. Activating makes use of experience and utilises tools or processes that are readily available or tried and trusted. Activating has an immediate impact on things, injecting a sense of urgency, and aiming to achieve clear goals and high-quality, tangible results.

On the next pages you will find a fuller description of each of these roles illustrating the behaviours and contributions that each can make to a team…

"When someone is clarifying, they are trying to bring clarity to the inner world of information and ideas".

Clarifying team members often spend time listening, asking questions and absorbing information, so that in their mind's eye they can achieve as clear a picture or understanding as is possible. Surety of knowledge and the reliability of experience are important to Clarifying team members, and a lot of their attention is directed towards building up their knowledge, and understanding their observations in terms of what they already know.

Clarifying team members also look to the future, but not in a speculative way. They often envisage clear goals, and clear pathways to achievement of those goals, on which they keep focused over a long period of time. That is, they do not work towards objectives that are vague or ambiguous, nor do they rely on a lot of guesswork in their implementation, but they try to understand the plans or processes by which a specific objective may be realised.

To the outside observer, because the Clarifying product is in the inner world of ideas and thoughts, it can sometimes seem that no contribution to the team is being made. However, internally clarity is being added to what is going on, discussions or tasks are related to known experience, and sure information is separated from mere speculation or guesswork. A Clarifying team member may speak infrequently, but what is articulated is often the product of much thought.

Clarifying team members often appear to have a good memory for lots of information. This may be a corollary of the depth of processing to which each piece of information is subjected: the more time is spent clarifying something, drawing out what is relevant and relating it to their experience, the more likely it is to be remembered.

When the team discusses the introduction of change, the main concern of Clarifying team members will often be to ensure the team defines the goals of that change, what it means, and the way it is to be achieved. To other, change-oriented team members this process can be mistaken as change-resistance. But when that clarity of definition is achieved, Clarifying team members can then be the most conscientious in implementing change. This is because they are often the ones who have the clearest view of what is involved, and retain that focus throughout the project. In fact, they may act as the team "anchor", preventing the team from losing sight of the original objectives.

If a team is deficient in the Clarifying team role, there may be a lack of continuity in the way work is undertaken. There may also be confusion resulting from the loss of vital information, and ambiguity over people's roles and objectives, or team decisions.

Clarifying team members are most effective when they are clarifying information, relating it to their experience and expanding their understanding. Their experience can often be a significant resource to the team, and brings a sense of continuity. Their creativity can be hindered when the discussion seems to be rambling and the team is going from one tangent in the discussion to another.

analysing

"When someone is Analysing, they are trying to understand and explain how things happen and why".

Analysing team members introduce structure and organisation into the inner world of ideas and understanding. They analyse ideas, and formulate hypotheses and explanations of how things function. They produce mental models that replicate how a particular aspect of the world works, or determine the principles and laws that identify the relationship between cause and effect.

Analysing team members formulate questions or hypotheses, gather evidence, and compare or analyse different ideas and viewpoints. They spot flaws or inconsistencies and test out the differences to find out which is true. They often try to understand the full complexity of the problem or situation being considered.

Analysing team members structure and organise ideas in an analytical or systematic way. When they interact with others, it is often by engaging in logical debate. If they are expected to modify their views significantly, to accommodate the feelings or sensitivities of others, this may feel as if they are being asked to sacrifice the truth. When they present their ideas, they usually want the team to engage in a rational discussion of their validity.

Analysing team members' analytical approach can extend to many areas, including the way in which the team operates. Whereas other team members may just accept and operate team processes, Analysing team members may analyse the relationship between those processes and team performance. This can give the impression that Analysing team members are not team players, or that they are critical of the team, but this is often a misinterpretation of their intentions: they are making an analytical contribution to the team by identifying how team effectiveness can be improved.

Analysing team members often seem to be collectors of information, as they formulate many questions and seem to absorb many facts or ideas. However, their interest lies not in information for its own sake, but what it tells them about the truth or accuracy of the hypotheses and explanations they are forming. They use the facts to help determine how things work.

The end product of Analysing team members' thinking is often a new idea or insight, which may seem to overlap with the Innovating team role (which involves coming up with new ideas). However, whereas Innovating uses imaginative intuition to dream up new ideas, Analysing uses logic to construct new ideas by a process of analysis and synthesis.

If a team is deficient in the Analysing team role, it may find it hard to explain why problems occur which makes it hard to find appropriate solutions and can result in the implementation of solutions that have little chance of success.

Analysing team members are most effective when they are allowed to grapple with the complexity of the principles involved in a situation. Their creativity can be hindered if they have to make significant compromises in what they believe to be right, in order to avoid causing offence.

"When someone is Innovating, they are using their imagination to create new and different ideas and perspectives".

For Innovating team members, the starting point can be their observation of the world around them. It acts as a springboard from which their imaginations embark on an internal brainstorm, from which comes a stream of new, creative and imaginative thoughts.

Innovating team members might ask themselves questions such as:

- "How can something be used differently?"
- "Can this be viewed from a different perspective?"
- "Is there a radically new solution to this problem?"
- "Is there an alternative meaning that can be attributed to what is seen?"

Innovating team members often demonstrate an apparent understanding of what cannot be clearly known. For example, the long term future can rarely be known for certain, but Innovating team members imagine how that future might be. To some members of the team, this can appear as guesswork and wild speculation, but to someone who is Innovating it is vision, insight, or an awareness of long-term strategy.

Innovating team members are most interested in those ideas or thoughts that have the greatest amount of potential. They often generate lots of new ideas, new possibilities, new themes, new strategies, and new goals. They see hidden connections between ideas and concepts that others may not have seen. However, Innovating team members may not express their views to others until they have finished developing their train of thought - at which point it is only the final and best idea that may be articulated.

Any situation or team discussion can spark a stream of imaginative ideas within the Innovator, the final product of which is a thought or idea that is far away from the original discussion. Whilst the idea can be of great value, when it is articulated, it can sometimes be difficult for the team to see the immediate connection between it and the original discussion.

Innovating team members often see a multiplicity of meaning in what they observe, interpreting things symbolically in different ways, depending on the different perspectives they take. This contrasts with the approach of Clarifying team members, who seek to clarify the 'singular' meaning of information or signs.

If the team is deficient in the Innovator team role, it may take a blinkered view on its work. This may result in an absence of innovation, a failure to see things from anything other than their own perspective, or focusing on the short term at the expense of strategy.

Innovating team members are most effective when they have the freedom to consider many different ideas and perspectives. It would hinder their creativity to restrict them to short-term fixed objectives that have known solutions. That is, they may find it inhibiting if the team seems to take a purely pragmatic or short-term approach.

"When someone is Campaigning, they are focussing on what is important about particular ideas, thoughts or beliefs".

Campaigning team members build harmony in the inner world of ideas and thoughts. That is, they want their thoughts and ideas to 'feel right' - and what makes ideas feel right is whether they are in accord with the person's beliefs and values.

Campaigning team members are therefore value driven, and in a team discussion, they often bring a sense of priority that is derived from their strong convictions. They seize upon and emphasise ideas or thoughts that have the greatest import, bringing them to the fore and stressing their significance.

Campaigning team members therefore notice, and bring to other people's notice, what they view as the inherently important issues. When they encounter new ideas or thoughts, they assess their value or importance, and then concentrate on those things about which they feel most strongly or passionately. Ideas or thoughts that are of little inherent value or regarded as unimportant are paid much less attention, being allowed to drift out of focus, or even deliberately pushed to the back of their minds.

Campaigning team members often do best in situations that allow them to emphasise, promote or support those ideas or beliefs about which they have passionate views. They may find a role frustrating or demotivating if it involves pursuing work that they see as having no meaning or value.

Campaigning team members may expect other team members to adhere to what the Campaigner regards as the team's core values but, if they don't, this can lead to unexpected conflict. Whilst they are often concerned to have positive working relationships, and are therefore adaptable to the wishes of other members of the team, this adaptability does not take priority over their values. For relatively unimportant issues, Campaigning team members can be very accommodating, but when it comes to their strongest convictions, they may go to extraordinary lengths to fight for what they believe in.

If a team is deficient in the Campaigning team role, then it may lose its sense of focus and drift from its core business, corporate identity or key objectives. Although work may be 'prioritised' (put into sequence), the team tries to achieve too much, to the extent that team performance suffers because its efforts are spread too thin. Also, key messages may be lost in the general volume of information – for example, the marketing messages conveyed to customers might be somewhat confused and undermine any sales efforts.

Campaigning team members are most effective when they are able to devote time and thought to things and beliefs that they value. It would be a hindrance to their creativity to force them to adhere to a predetermined structure or for them to undertake work that has no apparent purpose, value or meaning for them.

"When someone is Harmonising, they are trying to build agreement and connection with the people around them based on shared values".

Harmonising team members build a rapport with people, create a positive team atmosphere, look after people's welfare, or provide a service to the satisfaction of others. They often want the team and/or situation to 'feel right', so that people feel motivated, and positively disposed towards the team, their work, the service being given, or the product being produced.

Harmonising team members value other people's contributions, and often seek to nurture or develop the role that others play. They also invest a lot of effort in building positive relationships with their colleagues or customers. They try to overcome differences of opinion and find ways in which the team can agree. They seek accord, so that the team are working together, rather than pulling in their own different directions.

Harmonising team members work best in environments where there is a good team spirit, and positive working relationships - and relationships are often the focus of their attention. They often expect other members of the team to place a high priority on co-operation and teamwork, and not allow individual conflicts to damage working relationships.

They are likely to find a team frustrating to work in if it consists of independently-minded individuals who seem to be more concerned with defending their own ideas, rather than working harmoniously together.

Harmonising team members tend to show a high degree of concern for people and demonstrate a lot of interest in the welfare of others and how they feel. When they find themselves in a situation of conflict with someone, they aim to win the other person over and re-establish a positive working relationship. Harmonising team members also try to keep in touch with people with whom they have built a good relationship, even when the work no longer demands any contact.

Harmonising team members' desire for harmony is not limited to people, but also applies to things and situations. They often put a lot of effort into creating a pleasant working environment, and into fulfilling their job obligations so that they feel good about their work.

If the team is deficient in the Harmonising team role, inadequate attention will be paid to developing genuinely positive relationships, both within and outside the team. This can result in the absence of an effective network, making it more difficult to win the co-operation of others. It can also result in a more political work environment where people give priority to their own agendas.

Harmonising team members are most effective when dealing with people in a positive atmosphere, based on genuinely good relationships. It can be a hindrance to their creativity if they have to work in isolation, have to deal purely with the analysis of ideas, systems and impersonal data, or if their job requires that they be in constant conflict with others.

"When someone is Exploring, they are trying to find new and better ways of doing things, or trying to uncover potential in people, things or situations".

Exploring team members are often looking one step beyond the current situation - trying to find new and better possibilities than are immediately apparent.

Exploring team members often break new ground and pursue unexplored avenues with vigour until all the possibilities have been exhausted, or all the potential identified. They often challenge the status quo and experiment with the introduction of change, to see if the situation can be improved or some new potential uncovered.

Exploring team members tend to operate in situations that are novel and unique, and where the ground rules are few - they try things out and see what happens. If things don't work out, they change their decisions and try something better. They often initiate new work or projects that have potential, without necessarily having defined the specific goal - this will emerge through a prototyping or evolutionary approach that develops and refines the final outcome.

In areas where there are proven, reliable solutions, Exploring team members may introduce change to see if things can be done even better. Whereas some team members may wish to see the benefits demonstrated before change is introduced, Exploring team members introduce change as a way of finding out what the benefits might be.

Exploring team members are often willing to try new team processes, putting a lot of effort into them to see if team effectiveness can be improved. They work better with general guidelines rather than detailed procedures - because processes that are tightly defined restrict their ability to experiment with better ways of doing things.

In social situations, Exploring team members often build rapport with people through the inherent interest of the various topics that they discuss. They can take conversations off at tangents into new areas – and, as a result, two Exploring team members can go through many topics in just a few minutes!

If the team is deficient in the Exploring role, it may get stuck in a rut and fail to introduce change when it is appropriate. The team may fail to recognise and exploit any new opportunities that the situation presents.

Exploring team members are most effective when they have the headroom and flexibility to try things out, to see what lies around the corner, or look for what can be done to create something better in future. Their creativity can be hindered when they are constrained to working towards detailed, specific objectives that restrict their ability to try something new.

"When someone is conducting, they are trying to bring organisation and structure into the way things are done".

Conducting team members organise the world around them in a logical and structured fashion. They establish plans, identify appropriate procedures, and implement them. They try to ensure that roles and responsibilities are properly defined and that resources are available to undertake the work assigned.

Conducting team members establish logical connections between people and things. They sometimes draw comparisons between situations, identifying the similarities, differences or contradictions, and using the comparisons to determine the most correct way of doing things. For example, when embarking on a new project or task, Conducting team members may ask how other teams deal with similar situations, and what processes they use. Conducting team members then incorporate the best processes from these teams into their own work or within their own team.

Conducting team members contribute their best in areas where efficiency and effectiveness can be greatly enhanced through better planning or organisation. They systematise activities so that the goal can be achieved in an orderly manner.

Team processes are often quite important to Conducting team members, as they provide coherence in what could potentially be a chaotic, unstructured and ineffective team. In the absence of team processes, Conducting team members may step in and create them.

Conducting team members' working relationships tend to be organised on a professional and business-like basis - where the boundaries of responsibility and competence are recognised, and each person fulfils the role that is expected of them. Friendships tend to emerge from mutual respect based on competence.

Conductors' decisions tend to be guided by what is the correct or logical thing to do in a situation.

If the team is deficient in the Conductor team role, team members may be uncoordinated and lack common standards in their work. The team may not have sufficient structure and organisation, and may end up working inefficiently, duplicating effort or not being as effective as they could be.

Conducting team members tend to be most effective in situations that need to be logically structured and organised. It might hinder their creativity if they have to compromise too much for emotional reasons, or rely on constant improvisation. They may find it inhibiting if they have to operate in situations where individual freedom is paramount, and the situation is so unstructured that there is nothing that can be systematised.

"When someone is Activating, they are trying to bring things to fruition – getting things done, and getting them done now!"

Activating team members are very action-oriented. They tend to take an immediate view of the situation, seeing what needs to be done and getting on with it. They work towards tangible products and clear goals - ones that they know from experience can be achieved, or that can be clearly visualised from the outset of their work. They tend to use tools or processes of which they already have some knowledge, rather than use untried or experimental methods with unknown outcomes

Activating team members not only take action themselves, but they often spur others into action as well. They introduce a sense of urgency, working energetically to make progress, and generate useful or productive effort.

Activating team members tend to focus on problems or tasks that are inherent in the current situation, and they try to have an immediate impact on things. If an urgent problem presents itself, then Activating team members respond in kind and deal with it. Examples of the types of situations that bring out an Activating response are fire fighting, problem solving or sales.

Because Activating team members' main priority is achievement of the task, they are likely to appreciate having tools and techniques readily available that can be picked up and used 'in the heat of the moment'. They can achieve a lot when they are provided with support from people who have a 'can-do' attitude and are focused on the same goals. On the other hand, any team processes that seem to inhibit achievement may be ignored or even resisted.

Whilst Activating team members are often ready to embrace change, they tend to trust their experience and knowledge, and therefore opt for the solutions they know will work. For any new or innovative approaches, they will need to be convinced of the benefits - and a "convincing argument" is one where there is a clear demonstration that the new approach will be better and will work.

In social situations, Activating team members often bring experiences to life, for themselves and for others - e.g. telling anecdotes that illustrate interesting aspects of life, or introducing people to activities or sports that make life more exciting.

If the team is deficient in the Activating team role, they may spend too much time on background activities and fail to put sufficient energy into achieving the immediate tasks in hand. Too much time may be spent on discussion, and insufficient effort put into taking action.

To be most effective, Activating team members need to be given freedom to address issues as and when they arise. Their most creative contribution is in bringing things to fruition. Hindrances to that creativity include being closely supervised, having to work within a restrictive structure, or having to lay aside short-term imperatives in favour of developing long-term strategy or speculative ideas.

A Team-Role based methodology for Team Decision-Making

The 8 team roles not only provide a description of the key activities and behaviours that are likely to make a team successful, they also provide a sequence that can introduce discipline to a team. This is particularly important for teams when they lose focus or do not seem to be making progress. It is also a good discipline to reduce the risk of forgetting to do things, following the impulse of the moment or being led (sometimes inappropriately) by the loudest or most influential. This sequence is as follows:

1. **Clarifying**
   - Clarify the problem or decision to be made
   - Collect facts and information that relate to the problem
2. **Analysing**
   - Analyse the problem to identify the cause
   - Identify any related situations where this problem/issue may have been encountered before
3. **Innovating**
   - Come up with alternative solutions to the problem
   - Allow all ideas to be aired, no matter how radical
4. **Campaigning**
   - Consider the value of each idea and decide with to accept/reject
   - Prioritise those ideas, identifying the solution that is preferred
5. **Harmonising**
   - Consider who else needs or would want to be involved
   - Consider how to win their commitment/involvement
6. **Exploring**
   - Try out or pilot the chosen solution to see what impact it has
   - Sound out other people on the proposal to see how they react

7. **Conducting**

- Identify plans of how to implement the chosen solution
- Identify resources, responsibilities and timescales

8. **Activating**

- Take action to bring the chosen solution to fruition
- Tackle unexpected implementation problems as they arise

The Team Decision-Making sequence

In terms of the Type Mapping wheel this sequence is shown with the arrows:

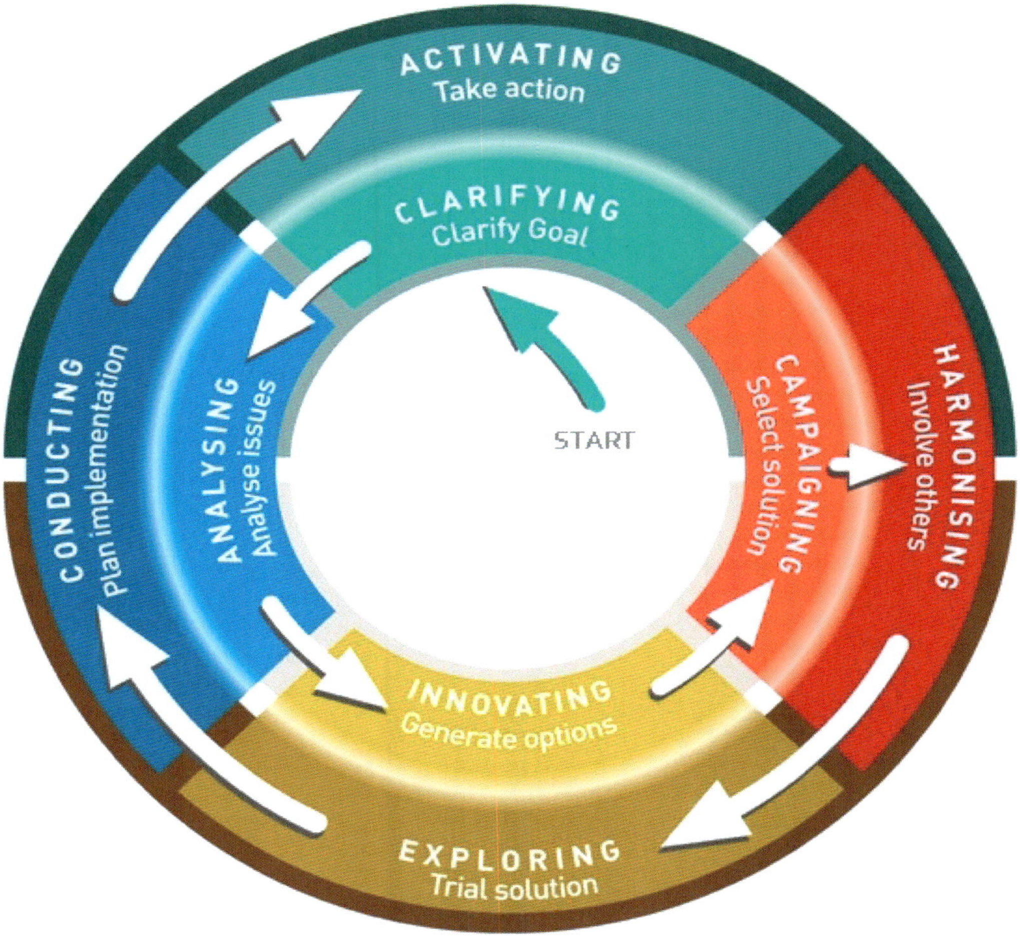

A team that uses this model learns to manage itself according to the demands of the situation and task rather than relying on the personalities of the team members – which can reduce the 'Ricochet Team Effect' (i.e. the bouncing about of the loudest voices and the biggest egos). It also focuses people on behaviour that can be managed and changed rather than personalities that are often viewed as less flexible.

ISBN 978-0-9934169-2-7

Printed in Great Britain
by Amazon

52317692R00022